Fascinating Food Chains

City Food Chains

By Julia Vogel

Illustrated by Hazel Adams

Content Consultant
Jacques Finlay, PhD
Assistant Professor
Department of Ecology, Evolution, and Behavior
University of Minnesota

magic Wagon

visit us at www.abdopublishing.com

Published by Magic Wagon, a division of the ABDO Publishing Group, 8000 West 78th Street, Edina, Minnesota 55439. Copyright © 2011 by Abdo Consulting Group, Inc. International copyrights reserved in all countries. All rights reserved. No part of this book may be reproduced in any form without written permission from the publisher.

Looking Glass Library™ is a trademark and logo of Magic Wagon.

Printed in the United States of America, North Mankato, Minnesota.
042010
092010

Text by Julia Vogel
Illustrations by Hazel Adams
Edited by Nadia Higgins
Interior layout and design by Nicole Brecke
Cover design by Kazuko Collins

Library of Congress Cataloging-in-Publication Data
Vogel, Julia.
  City food chains / by Julia Vogel ; illustrated by Hazel Adams.
     p. cm. — (Fascinating food chains)
  Includes index.
  ISBN 978-1-60270-791-7
 1. Urban ecology (Biology)—Juvenile literature.
 2. Food chains (Ecology)—Juvenile literature.
 I. Adams, Hazel, 1983- , ill. II. Title.
  QH541.5.C6V64 2011
  577.5'616—dc22
                              2009050436

Table of Contents

A City Food Chain

A food chain tells us who eats what. It shows how living things need each other. Let's find out what's for dinner in the city!

In one city food chain, a dandelion comes first. A woolly bear caterpillar chomps on the plant's leaves. But the caterpillar is also good to eat. A house wren catches it in its beak. Then, high above, a bigger bird is on the hunt. Down swoops a peregrine falcon and attacks the wren.

Dandelion to caterpillar to wren to falcon. That's a simple food chain. But a rabbit hops along and also nibbles on the dandelion leaf. Another food chain begins. When many food chains connect, they make food webs.

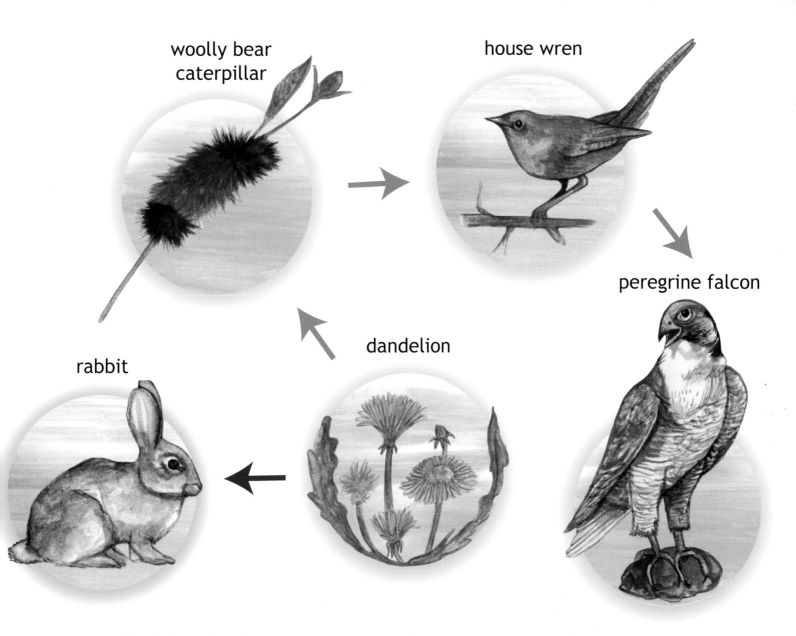

woolly bear caterpillar

house wren

peregrine falcon

dandelion

rabbit

Food gives living things the nutrients and the energy they need to live. The arrows show which way nutrients and energy move through the food chain.

5

Noisy, Busy City

In cities, buildings line the streets. Roads crisscross everywhere. Streetlights blink at every corner.

There seems to be little space left for wild animals. But pigeons and other creatures can still find food and water. In this noisy, busy world, plants and animals are linked in surprising food chains.

New York City is the largest city in the United States. More than 8 million people live there, along with pigeons, falcons, and other animals.

Plants Come First

Plants are the first link in a city food chain. That's because they make their own food. Plants live off water and sunlight. They also need space.

In the city, people plant trees and flowers in parks and gardens. Weeds, such as dandelions, find spaces on their own. These hardy plants can even grow in sidewalk cracks.

Many city plants came from faraway places. Dandelions came from Europe and Asia. Long, tough roots help them survive in cities around the world.

9

Herbivores Eat Plants

Dandelions in city parks make a feast for a woolly bear caterpillar. A groundhog finds a thin patch of green and starts munching. These animals are herbivores. They eat plants. They are the next link in the food chain.

Like plants, city herbivores must find space among the crowds of people and buildings. Lettuce leaves in a small city garden are dinner for a rabbit.

Carnivores Eat Meat

A house wren weighs less than two nickels. But it can snatch a caterpillar off a dandelion leaf. It flies off and eats its dinner on a rosebush. Nutrients and energy from the leaf the caterpillar ate go into the wren.

Animals that eat other animals are called carnivores. In the city, carnivores are often small. They are the next food chain link.

Ladybugs are carnivores. They eat aphids, which are tiny insects that feed on rosebushes.

14

During the day, many city animals hide to stay safe. When people go inside at night, these animals come out. Bats fly out of attics to chase moths. Rats crawl from tunnels to dig through garbage. Cats slip outdoors to catch mice. Animals that are active at night are called nocturnal.

Many bats use their ears to hunt in the dark. They make high-pitched squeaks that bounce off bugs. Echoes from the squeaks tell bats where to find their prey.

Top Carnivores Rule

A wren that eats a caterpillar is a carnivore. Then a peregrine falcon swoops down from a skyscraper. The powerful bird snatches the wren.

The falcon is a top carnivore. It hunts other meat eaters. Top carnivores rule city food chains. Usually, nothing eats these fierce hunters.

Omnivores Have Lots of Choices

A raccoon climbs a tree to steal chicks from a wren's nest. But it will also swipe tomatoes from a garbage can. It is an omnivore. It eats both meat and plants.

Food may be hard to find in cities. An animal that eats only one kind of food might starve. But hungry omnivores find lots of food.

Before pigeons lived in cities, they ate mostly seeds. But like most city animals, pigeons now are not picky. They might eat a dropped hot dog as well as seed at a bird feeder.

Homeless pets are often city scavengers. Without an owner to care for them, they may often be hungry. A rabbit killed by a car may be the best meal a lost dog or cat can find.

The Dead Get Eaten

The raccoon wanders along through the night. It finds a dead bird to eat. A rat eats a young pigeon that fell from a skyscraper nest. Raccoons and rats are scavengers. They feed on dead things. In cities, they are like a crew of animal street cleaners.

The raccoon is full and wanders off. Now other creatures will have their turn on the leftovers. Cockroaches, fly larvae, and tiny bacteria are decomposers. They break down dead things. They also feed on waste.

Decomposers clean up waste. As they do, they return nutrients to the soil, helping city plants grow.

In the city, decomposers often don't get a chance to help the food chain. They get thrown away—along with the garbage they consume.

People and the Food Chain

As long as people have lived in cities, they have been part of city food chains. Ancient Mayans grew vegetables and fruit trees in city gardens. Early New Yorkers raised chickens in pens and let hogs loose in the streets. People are omnivores in city food chains.

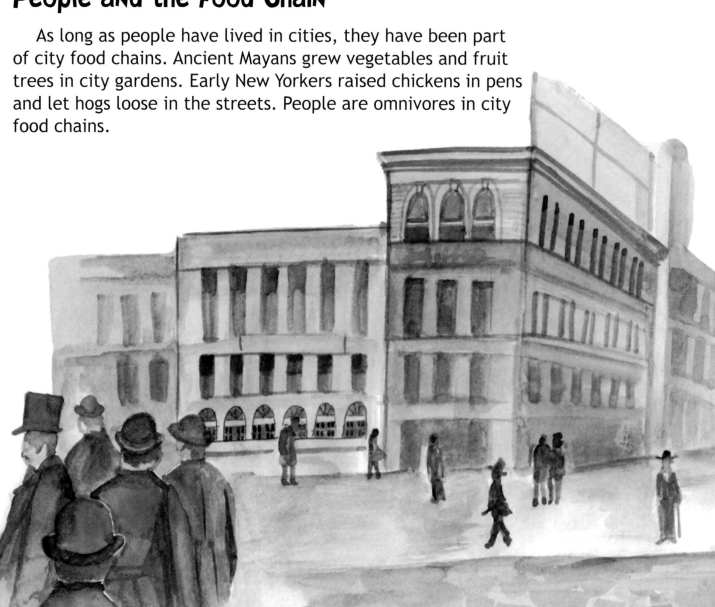

People change city food chains in many ways. They may cut down trees to build more roads. They may dump harmful chemicals that poison a city stream. These actions take food away from animals.

But people do helpful things, too. They fill bird feeders with sunflower seeds. They plant garden flowers that feed butterflies and hummingbirds.

Many people feed birds for a fun hobby. Finches and other birds visit city yards to eat corn and seeds. But if spilled seed is not cleaned up, rats and other pests may come at night for a meal, too.

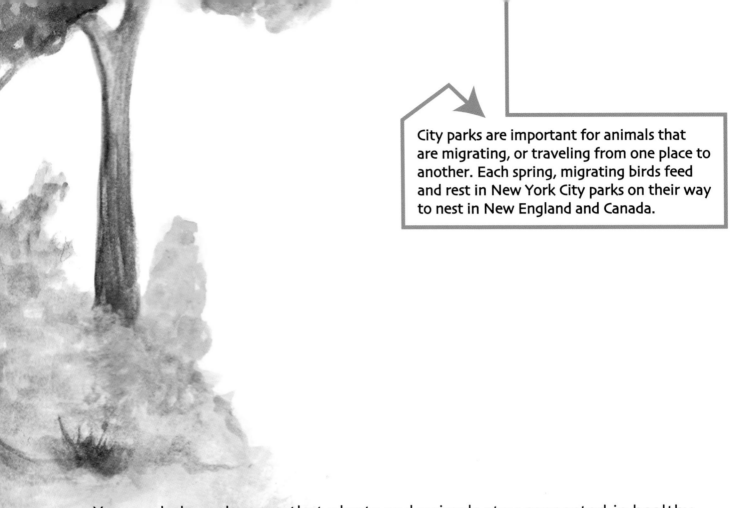

City parks are important for animals that are migrating, or traveling from one place to another. Each spring, migrating birds feed and rest in New York City parks on their way to nest in New England and Canada.

You can help make sure that plants and animals stay connected in healthy food chains. Never dump chemicals that could poison a city stream. Feed pets inside, and clean up garbage spills to avoid feeding rats. Plant trees and flowers on balconies and rooftops.

Most important, learn as much as you can about green spaces in cities. Tell others how important and interesting city food chains are!

Food Chain Science

Scientists study city food chains and food webs. They want to learn about all the ways plants and animals are connected.

In the 1960s, peregrine falcons in the United States were disappearing because of pollution. In 1970, scientists began to address the problem. They collected falcon eggs and raised birds indoors to keep them safe.

Later the researchers decided to try setting some birds free. In early experiments, young peregrines were released on cliffs where their parents once nested. Many were eaten by great horned owls and other predators.

Scientists also looked to Europe for an example. Peregrines there had also nested on tall church towers. So the next experiments set birds free in U.S. cities. With few large owls around, more young peregrines survived. Flocks of pigeons kept them well fed, and the peregrines grew up to nest and raise young of their own.

Peregrine falcons now perch on towering rooftops, scanning great cities for prey. By understanding the birds' place in food chains, scientists discovered that cities can sometimes help wild animals survive.

Fun Facts

Raccoons often rely on touch to decide what to eat. Their sensitive front paws feel an object all over to make sure that it is good food.

Peregrine falcons are the fastest animals in the world. They capture pigeons and other birds from the air, diving 200 miles per hour (322 km/h) to snatch their prey.

The world's largest urban bat colony is in Austin, Texas. There, 1.5 million bats roost under a bridge. They fly out at night to catch bugs in the Texas sky.

Streetlights can change a city food chain. If a light attracts moths and other insects, bats may swoop in to catch the bugs.

Restaurants, apartments, and other buildings crawl with cockroaches. Roaches will eat almost anything, including cookie crumbs, toothpaste, bacon grease, and pigeon poop.

Pet cats kill millions of small animals every year. They eat mice, wrens, and other prey that owls and other wild predators need to stay alive.

Tourists in Venice, Italy, used to buy corn to feed huge flocks of pigeons. But pigeon droppings are damaging old buildings and polluting water. To shrink the flocks, the city passed laws against feeding pigeons.

People usually think of coyotes as creatures of the Wild West. But the animals have spread to many eastern cities. They have even been spotted in New York City's Central Park.

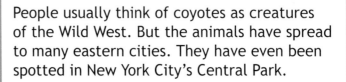

Words to Know

bacteria - tiny living things that help break down dead plants and animals. Bacteria can only be seen with a microscope.

carnivore - an animal that eats another animal.

decomposers - tiny living things that live on the dead remains of plants and animals as well as animal waste.

energy - power needed to work or live.

herbivore - an animal that eats plants.

nocturnal - active at night.

nutrients - chemicals that plants and animals need to live.

omnivore - an animal that eats plants and animals.

scavenger - an animal that eats dead animals.

top carnivore - a carnivore that is not preyed on by other carnivores.

On the Web

To learn more about city food chains, visit ABDO Group online at **www.abdopublishing.com**. Web sites about city food chains are featured on our Book Links page. These links are routinely monitored and updated to provide the most current information available.

Index